To my mother

Composer's World

Franz Schubert

by Wendy Thompson

VIKING

Introduction

On March 29, 1827, the body of Ludwig van Beethoven was laid to rest in the village cemetery of Währing, outside Vienna. Among the torch bearers in the funeral procession was a small, stocky young man of thirty, with curly dark hair and spectacles. Although Franz Peter Schubert lived in the same city as Beethoven all his life, he had only met the dying man for the first time the previous week. For him, carrying the torch was simply an act of private and public homage; but we can now see that it had a far deeper significance. The "torch" of Beethoven's genius had been passed on to Schubert — the last great Viennese composer of the late eighteenth and early nineteenth centuries.

Of the four famous composers who lived and worked in and around Vienna in what is generally called the Classical period, the oldest, Joseph Haydn, lived the longest. He died in 1809 at the age of seventy-seven. Mozart died when he was only thirty-five, less than half Haydn's age. The fifty-six-year-old Beethoven reached middle, if not old age; but Schubert's life was to be the shortest — and perhaps the most tragic — of all. Less than two years after he attended Beethoven's funeral, Schubert was buried, as he had wished, close to Beethoven in the Währing cemetery. He was only thirty-one.

But into that short lifetime he packed more work than most people manage in seventy years. His incredible list of compositions includes over 600 songs, several operas, masses and other music for the church, nine symphonies, and a large amount of chamber and piano music — over 1000 pieces altogether. These were all written in the space of only eighteen years, an average of more than one piece every week!

Although Schubert lived at exactly the same time as Beethoven, he was much younger, and his life was not so directly affected by the political upheavals that took place as the eighteenth century gave way to the nineteenth. He was only eighteen when the Napoleonic Wars ended, so his adult life was spent in the post-Napoleon era — the so-called "Biedermeyer" period, which describes a fashionable style of furniture and dress corresponding to England's "Regency" (the style of Jane Austen). The elaborate hairstyles, powdered wigs, beribboned dresses and lavishly gilded furnishings of the eighteenth century had disappeared in favor of simpler, more classic styles modeled on the Ancient Greeks and Romans; and many of the old, rigid class divisions had been swept away (there were now far more "middle-class" people, who could afford to live in relative comfort).

But postwar Vienna, where Schubert lived, was not a particularly pleasant place in some respects. The powerful politician Prince Metternich, who effectively ruled Austria, was a conservative who used his influence to fight against "subversive and revolutionary tendencies," such as the desire of ordinary people — especially the intellectual middle classes — for freedom and democracy. Metternich believed in a firmly established order of society in which the Church and the State were all-powerful. To preserve this "God-given" order, he introduced repressive measures to keep people under control, such as censorship of private letters, publications, and stage performances; compulsory registration; restrictions on travel (citizens had to obtain an official permit, even for holidays); and a fearsome network of spies and secret police. Schubert had several friends who

Friends meeting in a Viennese garden

dabbled in politics. One of these, a young man who had written articles criticizing the government, was arrested at a party, imprisoned for over a year without trial, and then exiled, his career ruined forever. Schubert was deeply shocked by his friend's misfortune.

To get away from all these petty restrictions, the people of Vienna spent as much time as possible enjoying them- selves. Balls and parties became very fashionable, and although a poor composer like Schubert could not afford to mix in aristocratic circles, he soon built up a circle of friends – poets and musicians – who often met at each other's homes and had "reading evenings," made music together, or visited the local pubs and coffeehouses.

Although Schubert inherited the Classical style in music

The poet J. C. F. von Schiller (1759–1805)

responded to these emotional poems by setting many of them to music. Unfortunately, songs were not then rated very highly in the musical world: they were regarded as "drawing room" music for entertainment. And unlike his three great predecessors, Schubert never held an official musical post at a court, or found an aristocratic patron to support him. He hoped to make a living by selling his music to publishers: he was one of the first entirely "free-lance" composers. (Mozart had tried to do the same thing in Vienna in the 1780s, and had failed.)

Schubert found life equally difficult: few publishers were willing to take the risk of publishing music by a young composer – however talented – whose name was relatively unknown outside Vienna, and whose works, especially the symphonies and the chamber music, seemed unfashionable. The age of the virtuoso performer had arrived, and people much preferred to flock to hear the stars of the day, such as the "wizard of the violin," Paganini, playing his flashy, brilliant but rather shallow music, than to attend a concert of "serious" chamber music which required intense concentration. Schubert did not live to enjoy fame or fortune. His towering genius, especially his inexhaustible gift for writing beautiful melodies, and his incomparable skill at setting words to music (which all composers of songs have since acknowledged) was not truly recognized until long after his death. "He was only a little man, but he was a giant," said one of his friends.

from Haydn, Mozart, and Beethoven, he was the first major composer of the new century, which is often known as the Romantic period in art. One of the key features of Romantic music is its strong association with literature or painting. Many of Schubert's finest pieces were inspired by the works of the leading German and Austrian poets of the time – Goethe, Schiller, Rückert, Klopstock, and Hölty. Such writers and poets did not concern themselves with the deeds of epic heroes from the past, but with the experiences and feelings of the ordinary person in real life: they spoke of love, happiness, sorrow, death, and the beauty of the natural world as anyone might experience them. Schubert

1 Childhood

Franz Peter Schubert was born on January 31, 1797, at a house known as "The Red Crayfish" belonging to the primary school in the Himmelpfortgrund ("gate of heaven"), a suburb of Vienna. His father, Franz Schubert (the name means "shoemaker"), was the headmaster of the school; and his mother, Elisabeth Vietz, was a locksmith's daughter from Silesia. Franz Peter was the twelfth of the couple's fourteen children, of whom, as often happened in those days, only a handful – four boys and a girl – survived childhood. The Schubert family's accommodation was very cramped; and shortly after the birth of their last child, Maria Theresa, in 1801, the Schuberts moved to a new house, with more rooms, nearby. There were no education authorities in those days, and the headmaster had to pay for his assistant teachers out of his own pocket, so naturally he preferred to employ his own sons where possible, to keep the money in the family. Franz Peter's elder brothers Ignaz and Ferdinand soon found themselves teaching, too.

Although Schubert's father was not a professional musician, he loved music. He played the cello, and he made sure that all his boys could play musical instruments. Ignaz and Ferdinand learned the violin, and Franz the viola, so that the family could play string quartets together for fun; and it was for these family practice sessions that Franz, during his school days, wrote about a dozen string quartets or quartet movements, together with sets of dances and other little pieces.

While Franz was growing up in this quiet suburb, the world outside was undergoing massive upheavals. By 1797 – the year of his birth – Austria was at war with France, where the ambitious young general Napoleon Bonaparte was beginning his campaign to dominate the world. An

The schoolhouse in the Säulenstrasse where Schubert was brought up

uneasy peace between the two countries ended in 1805, when Schubert was eight. The Austrian army was defeated at the Battle of Austerlitz, leaving 30,000 soldiers dead; and Napoleon marched into Vienna, taking over as his headquarters the Imperial family's summer residence, the beautiful palace of Schönbrunn. Emperor Franz was obliged to resign his official title of Emperor of Germany, and Austria was forced to give up many of her lands. Four years later, the Austrians rebelled, but were once more crushed, and Napoleon besieged Vienna with heavy artillery fire. The city walls were blown up, and the French again occupied the city. To persuade Napoleon to withdraw, the Emperor offered him the hand in marriage of his young daughter. Not until 1812, when the ragged, starving, and demoralized remnants of Napoleon's "Grande Armée" returned from his disastrous Russian campaign, did the citizens of Europe begin to feel that an end to the fighting might be in sight.

While all this drama was going on, young Franz Schubert was having his first music lessons from his father, and from Michael Holzer, the organist of the local parish church. Holzer drank rather too much, but he gave the boy a thorough grounding in organ, piano, violin, singing, and harmony. "He knew everything already," said Holzer. "I didn't need to teach him, only to watch him in silent aston-

Napoleon's troops arrive in Vienna, November 1805

A view of Vienna

ishment." In 1808, the newspapers announced a competition for a chorister's place at the Imperial and Royal Chapel, which also carried a free place at the Imperial and Royal Seminary (a kind of grammar school). Franz went for an audition; this meant he had to sing to the Imperial Kapellmeister, Antonio Salieri, an influential musician whose jealousy had done much to damage Mozart's career, but who had befriended the young Beethoven. To Franz's joy, he was accepted.

In October 1808, the eleven-year-old Franz went off to school, proudly wearing his new uniform – a low, three-cornered hat, a white neckerchief, a dark brown coat with a gilt epaulet on the left shoulder, polished buttons, an old-fashioned waistcoat, knickerbockers, and buckled shoes. He joined about 130 other boys, many of whom were the sons of army officers. All the music scholars took part in the services at the Imperial Chapel, and had daily music lessons. Franz took lessons in singing, piano, and violin. This gave him the opportunity to join the school orchestra (which played symphonies by Haydn, Mozart, and sometimes, even by Beethoven). The orchestra was run by a former pupil at the Seminary, Josef von Spaun, who by then was studying law at Vienna University. A talented violinist, Spaun loved music so passionately that during his own school days he spent all his pocket money on copies of the latest Beethoven symphonies, and he once had to walk all the way home to Linz at the end of term, because he had no money left for the coach fare. Spaun soon recognized young Schubert's ability as a violinist. He promoted him to leader of the first violins, and when Schubert, who was beginning to write his own pieces, confessed that he couldn't afford enough manuscript paper, Spaun bought him some. This was the beginning of a lifelong friendship.

Another school friend was a boy named Georg Eckel, who later became a famous vet. "He was shy and uncommunicative," recalled Eckel of Schubert. "He almost always spent his leisure hours in the music room, generally alone. . . Even on the walks which the pupils took together he mostly kept apart, completely absorbed in his own thought." But even so, Franz clearly had a sense of humor: on the manuscript of one of his early pieces he describes himself as "Franz Schubert, Chapel Master to the Imperial Chinese Court Chappppelll at Nanking!"

Although Franz's end-of-term reports were satisfactory, he soon seemed to be spending so much time on his music that his father was worried. He was not at all happy about the prospect of his son taking up music as a career. Then, in 1812, Franz's voice broke, and his mother died suddenly. Franz and his father agreed that he could stay on at school for one more year and continue with his music, so long as he paid attention to his academic studies. He also began to study harmony and counterpoint with the old Kapellmeister Antonio Salieri, who quickly recognized his talent. "That one knows everything," he said.

In his last year at the Seminary, Schubert wrote a great deal of music, including sets of minuets and German dances for orchestra, a drinking song for bass, chorus, and piano, 30 minuets for piano, an octet for wind instruments, several string quartets and his First Symphony. His work was so impressive that in November, he was recommended for an important scholarship. However, he would be expelled if he failed to get good marks in his academic subjects, since "singing and music are but a subsidiary matter." In the event, his mathematics let him down, and in November 1813, Schubert gave up his scholarship and left. His father had by then remarried, and needed help in the classroom. So the sixteen-year-old Franz returned home to become a teacher.

Joseph von Spaun (1788–1865), Schubert's lifelong friend

Right: *Vienna in the early nineteenth century*

VIENNA
(WIEN)

Published under the Superintendence of the Society for the
Diffusion of Useful Knowledge.

SCALES

English
Wien

French

NOTE.

Br. Brucke	Bridge	Hof	belonging to the
Eng. Englische	English	K.K.Koniglich	Kaiser Royal, Imperial
Font. Fontaine	Fountain	Mkt. Markt	Market
Gas. Gasse	Street	Neu. Neue	New
Gart. Garten	Garden or Park	Pl. Plats	Place or Square
Gr. Grosse	Great	St. Strasse	Street or Road
H. Haus	House	Thor	Tower

The City
has 12 Gates, Thoren, and 1257 Houses.
The Suburbs
are divided into 34 Vorstadte, with
10 Barriers, Leienthore, containing
6271 Houses. Total population 355,000.

2 The Schoolmaster

His duties in the schoolroom, teaching infants alongside his father and brothers for a miserable salary, did not tax Franz's imagination or capabilities very highly; but it did leave him plenty of time and energy for his music. In May 1814, he went to hear a performance of Beethoven's great opera *Fidelio* at the Kärntnerthor Theater, selling some of his books to raise enough money for the ticket. This experience inspired him to complete a stage work of his own, an operetta called *The Devil's Pleasaunce*, and his first major sacred work, a Mass in F major. The Mass was performed in the local parish church in October 1814. It was such a success that a second performance was arranged in the Augustine Church in the center of Vienna.

On both occasions, the solo soprano part was sung by the daughter of a family friend, a girl named Therese Grob, who was one year younger than Schubert. "She was no beauty, but well-shaped, quite buxom, with a fresh, childlike little round face, and a fine soprano voice," recalled one of Schubert's schoolfriends, who knew her well. "She is not particularly pretty, with a pockmarked face, but very good-natured," was how Schubert himself described her. But these rather negative terms (very similar to the way Mozart once described his fiancée) could not disguise the fact that Schubert had fallen madly in love with Therese. In October 1814, he began writing a series of songs, in which he tried to express his feelings. One of the best-known of these is *Gretchen am Spinnrade* ("Margaret at the Spinning Wheel"), which is based on a famous scene from Goethe's drama *Faust*, and it is the first real hint of Schubert's genius at painting a mood or an emotion in music. The brokenhearted Margaret, abandoned by Faust, sits sadly at her spinning wheel, whose monotonous revolutions are imitated in the

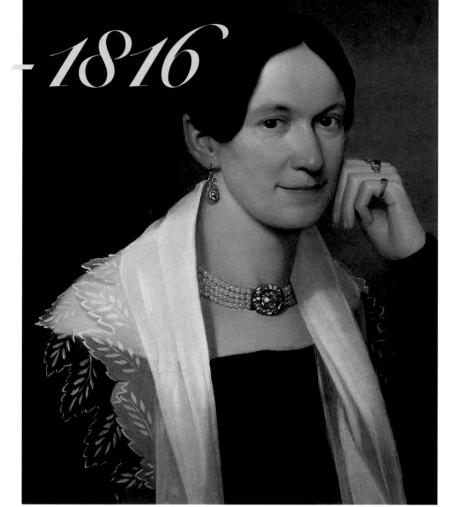

Therese Grob in later life

piano accompaniment, recalling the happiness of her meetings with her faithless lover. This famous song marked the beginning of Schubert's long and fruitful involvement with the poetry of Europe's greatest living writer, Johann von Goethe, whose work had a profound effect not only on literature, but on the whole of European culture in the early nineteenth century.

Schubert desperately wanted to marry Therese, but he was in no financial position to do so. Several years later she

Left: A plan of nineteenth-century Vienna

married a baker, but Schubert never forgot her. Instead, he found comfort in the company of his friends. In December 1814, Spaun introduced Schubert to the poet Johann Mayrhofer, who was then a law student in Vienna. Mayrhofer was a rather gloomy young man, with a sarcastic tongue: once his studies were finished he took a job in the Censorship Office, where he was responsible for vetting publications and people's correspondence. (This uncongenial job finally took its toll on his nerves: he committed suicide in 1836.) But he was a fine poet and a music lover, and he quickly became a close friend of Schubert, who set several of his poems to music. And in 1815, the "evil genius" of Schubert's life arrived on the scene – the charming, aristocratic, and flamboyant Franz von Schober, yet another law student at Vienna University. Although Schubert's own letters refer many times to his attraction to pretty girls, and indirectly, to his casual flings with them, it is now thought that some members of the Schubert circle were almost certainly "gay," among them Schober. In any case, it was probably Schober who introduced the modest and shy young composer to a kind of lifestyle which would eventually destroy him.

By his nineteenth birthday, Schubert's growing list of compositions included two more symphonies, two masses and other choral music, and music to accompany several plays, including one by Goethe, *Claudine von Villa Bella*. (After Schubert's death, the manuscript of *Claudine* was given to one of his close friends, whose servants accidentally

1814 – 1816

Franz von Schober (1796–1882)

12

Johann Mayrhofer (1787–1836)

used most of it to light the fire. Only Act One survived the flames.) And in one year alone, the tireless composer produced nearly 150 songs, including such gems as *Heidenröslein* ("The Hedgerose"), and the famous ballad *Erlkönig* ("The Erlking"). Both are based on poems by Goethe, but they could not be more different in tone. *Heidenröslein* is a simple little song in folk style, about a boy who goes to pick a rose from the hedge, but is severely scratched in the process; while *Erlkönig* describes a father's frantic ride through the forest at night, with his sick child in his arms, as he tries desperately to escape the clutches of Death, in the guise of the Erlking. Throughout the song, the horse's galloping hooves and the father's terror are represented by hammering triplets in the piano accompaniment.

Vignette from the title-page of "Erlkönig"

Johann Wolfgang von Goethe (1749–1832)

"Heidenröslein" (The Hedgerose)

By April 1816, Schubert had written so many songs based on Goethe poems that Spaun sent a set of twenty-eight to the great writer himself. Spaun explained that the young composer was intending to publish several sets of songs "to open his musical career," and respectfully asked permission to dedicate the Goethe settings to the poet "to whose glorious poetry he is indebted not only for the origin of many of them, but also, essentially, for his development into a German songwriter." Goethe didn't bother to reply: he merely returned the volume without comment.

Fortunately, Schubert wasn't discouraged: that year, he added another 100 songs to his list, including more Goethe settings, such as the immortal *Nur wer die Sehnsucht kennt* ("Only He Who Knows Longing") and *Kennst du das Land* ("Do You Know the Country") from Goethe's novel *Wilhelm Meister*; a setting of *Der Wanderer* (which later he was to use as the basis for his great piano work, the "Wanderer" Fantasy), and a delightful *Cradle Song*. He also wrote some dances for piano, and a cantata, *Prometheus*, for a private celebration in honor of Spaun's landlord. He received 100 florins for this piece, the first he had written "for money." And the following year he quickly completed two more symphonies, No.4 in C minor, known as the "Tragic"; and the sunny, elegantly lyrical Fifth Symphony in

B flat, which was performed by a private, amateur orchestra. Unlike Mozart, who wrote largely to commission, or Beethoven, who had his works professionally performed at "benefit" concerts, none of Schubert's early works was written with professional performance in mind — and in fact, he never heard even one of his symphonies played by a professional orchestra. Some of them, such as the Third Symphony, had to wait for over fifty years after his death before they were played in public. Schubert was essentially an "amateur" composer, writing for an ever-widening, but still relatively small, circle of middle-class, music-loving friends for whom music was an essential part of their home entertainment.

Schubert was now nearly twenty, and he was fed up with his life as a primary-school teacher. He had applied for a job as music master at a training college in Laibach (now Ljubljana in Yugoslavia), but had been turned down. In December, after three years at home (where space and quiet were impossible, thanks to the arrival of several little stepbrothers and sisters), Schubert left to take up lodgings with Franz von Schober, in the Landskröngasse.

The Josephsplatz, a square in Vienna, in Schubert's time

Andante con moto

3 Freedom

In March 1817, Schober introduced his shy young friend to the baritone Johann Michael Vogl, for many years a principal singer at the German Opera in Vienna. After an embarrassing start, during which Vogl wondered why he had been invited to meet this tongue-tied youth, he reluctantly agreed to sing through one of Schubert's songs. Immediately, Vogl realized that here was something quite extraordinary. He became one of Schubert's closest friends and supporters, tirelessly performing the young man's songs everywhere he went, and helping to get Schubert's name better known. And the songs kept pouring out: another sixty or so appeared in the year 1817, including *Der Tod und das Mädchen* ("Death and the Maiden") and *Die Forelle* ("The Trout"), both of which Schubert later used to provide themes for two of his greatest instrumental works; and the lovely *An die Musik* ("To Music"), which sets a poem by Schober. Schubert also completed no fewer than seven piano sonatas – works clearly influenced by Beethoven – between May and August the same year.

"An die Musik" (To Music)

By 1818, Schubert was back in the schoolhouse, prob-ably as his father's assistant. Because he was so short (he was just over five feet tall) and his sight was poor, he managed to avoid conscription into the army – something for which all men between eighteen and forty-five (unless they were in certain professions) were eligible – and the minimum term of service was fourteen years! Musical per-formers and composers were supposed to be exempted, but only if they could produce a certificate testifying to their professional status and qualifications. As yet, Schubert had nothing on paper to offer – but in February 1818, his first song was published. It was a setting of one of Mayrhofer's poems, *Erlafsee* ("Lake Erlaf"). And in the same month, an overture by Schubert was played by an amateur orchestra at a concert held in a small hotel in Vienna. It received encouraging reviews in the Viennese press: Schubert was praised for his "profound feeling," his "disciplined yet spon-taneous force," and his "appealing charm." This welcome public exposure led to another of his overtures being played at a concert a few months later; the critics liked the music, but the orchestra played out of tune.

Around the same time, a new symphony by Schubert, his sixth, which he described as a "Grand Symphony," was played in Vienna, once more by an amateur orchestra. Schubert's first five symphonies had all been small-scale works in the Classical mold of Haydn and Mozart; but from No.6 onward he began to expand the form just as Beethoven had done.

In 1818, Schubert was given a five-month travel permit to Hungary. He had found a summer job as music master to the two daughters of Count Esterházy of Galánta, a member of the same noble family for whom Haydn had worked for so many years. Count Esterházy and his family spent the summer on their country estate at Zseliz, about

100 miles east of Vienna. It was the first time that Schubert had left his native city. "I live and compose like a god," he wrote to his friend Schober. "Thank Heaven, I'm really living at last." Several fine works for his young piano pupils – a sonata, a set of variations (later dedicated to Beethoven "by his admirer and worshipper, Franz Schubert"), and

An anonymous portrait of Schubert

some dances, all for piano duet – were written at Zseliz. As was the custom, Schubert took his place among the other family servants: the bailiff, the rent collector, the doctor, the cook, the nurse, the caretaker, and the lady's maid, Pepi Pöckelhofer – "who is pretty and often visits me." Pepi was clearly pretty enough to make Schubert forget about his unhappy love for Therese Grob. But soon he began to feel lonely and homesick for Vienna, and he was glad to return to the capital in November.

The next summer, Schubert decided to take a holiday. He and his friend Vogl went to Steyr, a beautiful town about ninety miles west of Vienna. The house where they stayed in the attractive old marketplace is still there. Schubert went for long walks in the hills, flirted with the local girls, and enjoyed more than a few beers in the local taverns. He also found time to complete a piano sonata in A major, and to begin one of his most famous works – the "Trout" Quintet for piano and strings, which includes a set of variations on his song *Die Forelle*.

A view of Steyr in the nineteenth century

"Die Forelle" (The Trout)

By 1821, Schubert's reputation was growing, and his songs were being heard in the salons of Vienna's wealthy middle classes. On March 7 of that year, Vogl gave a performance of *Erlkönig* at a public concert at the Court Theater. The response was so enthusiastic that Schubert's friends arranged for it to be published. "For a week afterwards," wrote a member of the audience, "the whole town was talking about Schubert and his songs. People were falling over themselves to get hold of them." Unfortunately, Schubert was not much of a businessman, and in the flush of success he rashly sold the copyrights of ten whole books of his songs to the Viennese publisher Anton Diabelli. Thus ended any hope of future royalties from these songs, while Diabelli knew that he had done rather well out of the deal!

Meanwhile, Schubert's hopes of achieving success as an opera composer started to crumble. Italian opera, especially the works of the brilliant young composer Rossini, were now all the rage in worldly Vienna, while operas in German were considered dull and provincial. Encouraged by the warm critical reception given to two short comic operas he had written a couple of years earlier, Schubert had worked hard during 1821 on a full-length stage work,

Alfonso und Estrella. A friend of his was the director of the Court Opera, and he had promised Schubert a production. But in January 1822, his luck ran out: an Italian impresario took over the lease of the theatre, and Schubert's opera was rejected. Although he pressed on with two more stage works, a short comedy and *Fierabras*, a longer tale of Romantic chivalry, plans for their production came to nothing.

Altogether, Schubert tried his hand at about seventeen works for the stage – but nearly all were failures, and hardly any are heard today. He didn't seem to realize that he lacked Mozart's instinct for dramatic effect (something all great opera composers must possess), and he couldn't find a good enough story. His single success came in 1823, when he was asked to write some incidental music for a ridiculous "grand Romantic drama" called *Rosamunde, Princess of Cyprus* by an eccentric authoress, Helmina von Chézy. *Rosamunde* was performed twice at the Theater an der Wien, and Schubert's enchanting music – now one of his most popular and well-known compositions, on account of its memorable tunes – was well-received. Even two performances were better than none!

The Theater an der Wien,
where "Rosamunde" was performed

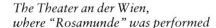

Entr'acte from "Rosamunde"

Andantino

4 Paradise Lost

In 1821, Schubert was twenty-four. His sociable nature had made him the focus of a close-knit group of talented young people – artists, poets, writers, students, and their sisters and friends – who enjoyed a happy and carefree existence: "a brilliant life," as one of them said. Just as the Parisian cafés of Montmartre and Montparnasse would later attract similar cliques of students, artists, musicians, writers, and philosophers – laughing, flirting, gossiping, drinking, and discussing serious issues of art and morality – so Vienna in the early nineteenth century was an ideal place for such social activities. It was a compact city, its spacious avenues well supplied with cafés and taverns, and surrounded by elegant parks and gardens in which citizens could stroll at leisure. Many jolly meetings took place during the after-noons in coffeehouses, such as Bognor's on the Singerstrasse, where clients could play billiards, cards, and chess, refresh themselves with soft drinks or liqueurs, smoke, read the newspapers, and exchange the day's gossip. In the evenings, Schubert and his friends either went to the local pubs for more serious eating and drinking, or else organized parties, known as "Schubertiads," at each other's houses. There they listened to poetry readings and to Schubert's latest music, played charades, acted out plays, and discussed love and politics. In the summer, they drove out to Atzenbrugg, a country estate managed by Schober's uncle, where they picnicked, drove around the countryside, and played ballgames. One of their number, the artist Leopold Kupelwieser, painted several charming watercolors of the social

Schubert and his friends playing ball at Atzenbrugg, by Kupelwieser

events at Atzenbrugg. But this idyllic existence was to come to an end: several members got married, while others left Vienna to pursue careers elsewhere, and the group gradually broke up.

And not all the activities of the Schubert circle were entirely innocent. Schubert himself was about to suffer a typically "Romantic" fate – William Blake's apt imagery of "the invisible worm that flies in the night" was soon to blight his whole existence, leaving him with only a few more years to live. His tragedy was closely bound up with the moral climate of the time.

In his day, young girls of good families were treated as marketable commodities – they had a marriage value. Until they were safely married off, they were closely guarded and chaperoned, especially in Catholic countries, where an unmarried girl's reputation had to be kept spotless. Middle-class women were not expected to work, so a potential suitor had to be able to prove to his prospective father-in-law that he could support a wife and family. For young musicians, artists, and writers – and indeed, anyone on an uncertain income, rather than a steady job – this was a great problem, and many middle-class young men simply couldn't afford to get married. Mozart found it impossible to persuade his own father that he could support a wife (and events proved that Leopold's judgment was not entirely wrong!) Such young men often tended to sow their wild oats with women of a lower class – servants, chambermaids – and prostitutes. "Biedermeyer" Vienna, despite a thin coating of morality, was actually a highly permissive city. Sex could be easily obtained, if you knew where to look, and visits to the brothel were considered quite normal. But the risks were great, as many people – among them several famous musicians – found to their cost.

By early 1823, Schubert realized to his horror that he

An excursion of the "Schubertians" from Atzenbrugg, by Kupelwieser

had contracted the worst form of venereal disease, syphilis. Then, like AIDS today, it was incurable and ultimately fatal. Penicillin, of course, was unknown, and the only treatment on offer was a course of mercury, which had painful and unpleasant side effects (it is itself a poison). By May, Schubert was in the hospital, and clearly wishing he were dead. But he struggled through, and after a summer holiday in Steyr, he began to recover physically, though he never again lost a strong feeling of self-disgust. One of his most famous works, the restless and tragic Eighth Symphony, which he never completed, was written just as his symptoms became obvious. Its existence clearly reminded the unhappy composer of his misery: he never took the slightest interest in it or attempted to have it published or performed.

Theme from the "Unfinished" Symphony

Playing charades at Atzenbrugg,
by Kupelwieser

But personal tragedy did not stem the flow of Schubert's creativity: at the height of his illness he finished the great "Wanderer" Fantasy for piano, a massive, virtuoso masterpiece based on a theme from the earlier song, *Der Wanderer*, and a new piano sonata, in A minor. At much the same time he composed his first major "song cycle" – a group of songs loosely linked together on a sequence of poems, telling a story. *Die schöne Müllerin* ("The Fair Maid of the Mill") is a typically Romantic tale of a young miller, who falls in love with his employer's daughter. For a while, his love is returned; but soon a rival appears in the person of a dashing gamekeeper. The rejected lover drowns himself in the millstream, which runs like a thread through the tragic romance – and is ever-present in the musical accompaniments to the songs.

Vignette from
the title-page of
"Die schöne Müllerin"

"Das Wandern" (To Wander) from "Die schöne Müllerin"

"The Raft of the Medusa" by Géricault

These twin themes – frustrated passion, often resolved only by death, and a response to Nature – are the hallmarks of Romantic literature. In the seventeenth and eighteenth centuries, Nature was regarded as an enemy, something to be tamed and stifled. Thus, in the great formal gardens of palaces such as Versailles, acres of "wilderness" were cleared to make way for straight rows of trees, color-matched flower beds, neatly trimmed hedges, elaborate terraces with artificial fountains and waterfalls, and "cultivated" hothouse plants alien to the natural environment. But in the Romantic era, writers and artists drew inspiration from Nature in her wilder, untamed, more "natural" moods. Géricault's famous painting "The Raft of the Medusa" (which caused such a scandal at its first exhibition in Paris in 1816), shows a raft of naturalistically painted corpses and dying men, adrift on a stormy sea, while Turner's "Fall of an Avalanche in the Grisons" (exhibited in 1810) vividly depicts the terrifying momentum of this natural phenomenon. This "back to Nature" movement started in late eighteenth-century France, influenced by novels such as *Émile* and *La Nouvelle Héloïse* by the French writer Jean-Jacques Rousseau. Rousseau rebelled against the artificial moral code of Classical writers and philosophers, who believed in a neatly ordered world in which everything was for the best. Later Romantic writers, such as Goethe, Byron, Shelley, and Sir Walter Scott, all identified human emotions with the turbulent moods of Nature. So Wordsworth drew his inspiration from the wild beauty of the Cumbrian landscape; while Shelley – one of the most intensely Romantic of English poets – achieved immortality not only through his verses, but by the way he died, drowned in a storm at sea, just like one of his own heroes.

Composers, too, began to depict landscapes and the natural world in their music: two of the most famous early nineteenth-century examples are Beethoven's "Pastoral" Symphony, which paints a musical picture of scenes in the countryside, including a storm and a peasant dance, and Mendelssohn's famous overture "The Hebrides," a vivid tone painting of the stormy Atlantic lashing the rocks behind Fingal's Cave, off the Scottish coast. Although *Die schöne Müllerin* did not make much impression at the time, Schubert's idea of making the millstream almost an equal partner in the drama was to have great influence on a whole generation of song composers who followed his example.

"The Fall of an Avalanche in the Grisons" by Turner

1821 – 1823

Schubert

A café in a Viennese park

5 Paradise Regained

By 1824, Schubert's friends had largely dispersed. Their reading parties had been taken over by a rowdy band of "beer-drinkers and sausage-eaters"; Schober had gone to Breslau to try to make his name as an actor; Spaun was away in Linz, and Schubert had fallen out with Mayrhofer. "I am the most unhappy and wretched creature in the world," he wrote to Leopold Kupelwieser, who had gone off to Italy. "Imagine one whose health has been permanently wrecked, and whom despair makes worse all the time; imagine one to whom the joys of love and friendship have nothing to offer but pain, who can no longer take pleasure in beautiful things, is he not the most unhappy of men? 'My peace is gone, my heart is sore, never shall I find it evermore' [a quotation from his song *Gretchen am Spinnrade*]." "I haven't written many new songs," continued Schubert, "but I have had a go at several instrumental works, two quartets for violins, viola, and cello, and an octet, and I want to write another quartet, which will, I hope, pave the way towards a grand symphony in that manner."

In such modest terms Schubert revealed that he had completed several of his finest chamber works, in a phenomenal burst of creative energy. "Schubert is looking much better," wrote a new friend, the painter Moritz von Schwind, to Schober. "He's very bright, ridiculously hungry,

and he's turning out quartets and German dances and endless variations. . . If you go to see him during the day, he says 'Hullo, how are you? Good' – and just carries on scribbling." The fruits of this period of absorption include the six-movement octet for wind and strings, written for an amateur clarinettist, Count Ferdinand Troyer, and deliberately modeled on Beethoven's popular Septet; and two exquisite quartets, one in A minor, and the other in D minor (known as "Death and the Maiden," since its slow movement is a set of variations on Schubert's song of that name). Unlike Mozart, who could turn out serenades and dance music of the most blithe and sunny nature even if he himself was in the depths of illness or depression, Schubert's state of mind clearly influenced his music, and all these works reflect to some extent the remark in his own notebook that "pain sharpens the understanding and strengthens the mind."

But a companionable person such as Schubert was never alone for long. He and several new friends, including

Caroline Esterházy
(1805–1851)
in later life

the young law student Eduard von Bauernfeld, continued to frequent the eating and drinking places of Vienna, especially the Café Wasserburg. In the summer of 1824, Schubert went once again to Zseliz, as music tutor to the Esterházy girls. Caroline was now a beauty of nineteen, and an affectionate relationship developed between teacher and pupil. Schubert wrote several piano duets for Caroline and himself to play, including the popular *Divertissement à l'hongroise* ("In the Hungarian Style"). But any serious relationship was clearly ruled out, and Schubert returned to Vienna in September, "well, delightfully silly, given a new lease of life by joy, pain and a pleasant existence," according to Schwind. There he completed a sonata for piano and arpeggione (an instrument like a cello, but with frets and six strings, now obsolete). The sonata is today often played on the cello or viola.

31

In February 1825, Schubert moved to the Wieden suburb of Vienna, to be closer to his "beloved" friend, Schwind. Schubert's songs were taken up by several famous singers of the day, including the Berlin soprano Anna Milder-Hauptmann (the first Leonore in Beethoven's opera *Fidelio*, a singer with a voice "as big as a house," so Haydn said, and with a figure to match); and several more compositions were published, including a Mass in C major, the A flat variations for piano duet, and some of his finest Goethe

Sig.ⁿ von Perger d. D.Weiß fc.

Pauline Anne Milder-Hauptmann

Opern=Sängerinn der K.K. Hoftheater.

Anna Milder-Hauptmann (1785–1838), *the famous singer*

The painter Moritz von Schwind
(1804–1871)

settings, such as *An Schwager Kronos* ("Kronos the Charioteer"), *An Mignon* ("To Mignon") and *Ganymede*. In the summer Schubert and Vogl went on a five-month tour of Upper Austria, visiting Steyr, Gmunden (a town on the shores of a beautiful lake, "the surroundings of which are truly heavenly," according to Schubert), Linz, the Salzkammergut, and "the famous, wild watering-place" of Gastein, with its magnificent waterfall. At Linz, they stayed with some relatives of Josef von Spaun. "Schubert was so friendly and communicative with all of us," wrote Spaun's brother-in-law. "I've never seen or heard him like this before: serious, profound, as if inspired. How he discussed art, poetry, his youth, his friends and the people who matter to him, of high ideals, and so on. What a mind!" This letter also mentions that Schubert was working on a symphony at Gmunden, which has led people to speculate that there was a lost symphony, called the "Gastein" or "Gmunden" Symphony. It is now known that Schubert turned these sketches into his last symphony, the "Great C Major."

A view of Gastein

A view of Linz in the early nineteenth century

By October, Schubert had returned to Vienna, to a joyful reunion with many of his former friends, and a resumption of the good old days. "Schubert is back," wrote Bauernfeld. "Inn and coffee-house gatherings with friends, up until two or three in the morning—

> With great shame, we must confess
> Every night
> Drinking and great laziness
> Bring us delight."

A view of Gmunden

Schubert in 1825, by W. A. Rieder

6 "A Divine Spark"

Schubert began the year 1826 with his last settings of poems by Goethe – Mignon's songs from *Wilhelm Meister*. He was clearly fascinated by the beautiful lyrics sung by the mysterious Italian child Mignon, who attaches herself and her strange traveling companion, the Harper, to the young poet Wilhelm Meister. Schubert had already set these verses once, but now he returned to them with renewed inspiration. By now, Viennese publishers, including the firm of Artaria (who had published works by Haydn, Mozart, and Beethoven), were competing with each other for Schubert's latest compositions, and several important piano and chamber works were published, including the famous *Marche Militaire*. But his reputation was still only a local one: when he approached the famous Leipzig firm of Breitkopf & Härtel, the firm replied politely that they might just consider publishing a piano piece, so long as the composer would accept free copies instead of a fee!

Money was always a problem for a composer without a steady job, and in April, Schubert's friends (who now included Spaun once more) persuaded him to apply for the job of vice-Kapellmeister of the imperial court chapel. But Schubert's lifestyle, especially his unpunctuality and inability to keep appointments, was not really suited to a proper job, with fixed working hours. He was probably secretly relieved – though still disappointed – when the post went to another composer.

In July, Schubert – by now getting rather portly owing to his frequent visits to the tavern, and known to his friends as "Tubby" – went to stay with Schober's relatives in Währing, just outside Vienna, where he wrote three of his best-known songs – settings of Shakespeare's *To Sylvia*, *Drinking Song*, and *Hark, Hark, the Lark*. (This last song was sup-

Allegro moderato

D.C. al ⊕
poi al Coda   CODA

36

A "Schubert Evening" at Joseph von Spaun's, December 1826, by Schwind (Schubert is accompanying the singer Vogl)

posed to have been jotted down in a café on the back of a menu-card, but there seems to be no truth in the story.) He also completed his last string quartet, in G major.

Two of Schubert's friends, Vogl (then well over fifty) and Leopold Kupelwieser, both got married in 1826. For those who were left, life went on during the autumn and winter in even more riotous fashion than before, with a never-ending succession of parties. The "Schubertiads" were reinstated: on December 15, there was one at Spaun's house, at which a "huge gathering" heard Vogl sing thirty Schubert songs, and the composer played piano duets with a friend.

"When the music was over," recalled a guest, "there was grand feeding and then dancing. . . At 12:30 . . . we went to the 'Anchor'. . . Merry. Then home." This memorable evening was later immortalized in a painting by Schwind. And the year ended on a similar note, after a snowball fight on leaving the pub the previous evening, during which Spaun fielded the missiles with his umbrella, the friends saw the New Year in at Spaun's house, smoking, drinking, "reading most amusing letters" and finally "waddling off" somewhat the worse for wear at two in the morning.

1826 - 1827

During January 1827, the parties continued unabated. On the 12th, after listening to a "splendid sonata for four hands, glorious variations and many magnificent songs," including *Erlkönig*, *Nacht und Traume* ("Night and Dreams") and *Die Abendrote* ("Sunset Glow"), everyone piled out "helter-skelter" to Bognor's, while Schwind impersonated a vampire, flapping his cloak and pretending to fly. And the following day, more "childish pranks" took place in the moonlight ouside Bognor's café, and round St. Stephen's Cathedral. But by March, Schubert was often absent: on the 4th, he invited his friends around, but never turned up himself. He was by then working on another song cycle, *Die Winterreise* ("Winter Journey"), another setting of poems by Wilhelm Müller. A young man leaves a village where the love and happiness he has known have turned to grief and desolation. He sets out alone, at the onset of winter, on a journey to nowhere. Croaking ravens and barking dogs shadow his departure. At the end, he throws in his lot with a traveling organ-grinder, whose repetitive music, attracting no attention, seems to symbolize the pointlessness of existence. The bleak, pessimistic tone of the new cycle shocked Schubert's friends, Schober hated the songs, and said so; but Schubert said he thought they were the best things he had ever written: "In time, you'll come to think so, too."

Toward the end of March, Schubert, who had always worshipped Beethoven from a distance, finally plucked up the courage to visit the dying composer. Beethoven had been given some of Schubert's songs – including part of *Die schöne Müllerin* – to look at on his deathbed. "Truly in Schubert there is a divine spark," he is said to have remarked. Carrying a lighted taper and a bunch of lilies tied to his arm with a black crepe band, Schubert took part in the master's funeral procession. After attending the funeral sermon and the burial, he and his companions returned sadly to their local taven, the "Castle of Eisenstadt," where they stayed up until 1 AM "talking of nothing but Beethoven."

The same year, Schubert found a new publisher, who issued several sets of songs and the G major Piano Sonata, an expansive, weighty work which came out under the friv-

Beethoven in 1824, by Stephan Decker

olous title of "Fantasie," since the publisher believed that the term "sonata" would put customers off! The work was extensively discussed in a review in the influential Leipzig *Musikalisches Zeitung* ("Musical Times"), in which the critic warned Schubert of the dangers of trying to emulate Beethoven, "one in a class of his own." In the summer, Schubert stayed at the village of Dornbach, not far from Vienna, where he may have written some of his charming piano impromptus; and later in the year he was invited by his friend Johann Baptist Jenger, a member of the Styrian Music Society, to visit Graz, in southern Austria. There he and his hosts enjoyed excursions to the surrounding countryside, including the castle of Wildbach, and held mini-Schubertiads, for which Schubert composed several dances known as the "Graz Galopp" and the "Graz Waltzes."

Graz: the main square in Schubert's time

Hauptplatz der Stadt Grätz.

Place principale de la ville de Grätz.

Schubert returned to Vienna in September, in poor health, suffering from severe migraine, and feeling rather depressed. "Vienna is empty of cordiality, candor, real thought, reasonable words and sensible deeds. There is so much confused chatter that everything is topsy-turvy, and it is impossible to achieve any inner contentment," he wrote. Even so, he was able to finish his song cycle *Die Winterreise*, and just as he had predicted, his friends gradually came to realize that they were hearing a masterpiece. "Schubert has understood his poet with his personal genius," reported a later review. "The emotions in the poems are faithfully reflected in his own feelings, and these are so manifest in sound that none can sing or hear them without being touched to the heart. . . Herein lies the nature of German Romantic being and art."

Schubert also began work on two massive piano trios, one of which, in E flat, was finished by December, and first performed by a trio which included the well-known Viennese violinist Ignaz Schuppanzigh, whose quartet had presented many of Beethoven's masterpieces to the world. The slow movement of the E flat Trio has a long drawn-out, poignant melody, heavy with anguish, but still one of Schubert's most beautiful creations. As an antidote to this great work, he also threw off a set of delightful, delicate piano miniatures called *Moments Musicaux*.

The slow movement of the Eb Piano Trio

7 Sunset Glow

After a long spell of remission, Schubert's illness was gradually taking its insidious toll of his health. But he went on composing – and socializing – feverishly, as if he knew that time was short. Josef von Spaun had become engaged, and to celebrate the occasion, the last Schubertiad, attended by over fifty people, took place at Spaun's house, at which members of the Schuppanzigh quartet played Schubert's new Trio, in B-flat major. The "circle" clearly approved of Spaun's fiancée, although she was "over thirty!" "We nearly all got tipsy," wrote one of the revelers. "We danced. . . then we nearly all went to Bognor's, where we sat on till 2:30."

In February, Schubert received an unexpected surprise. It was an offer from the Leipzig publishers Probst to consider "anything you have finished to your satisfaction – songs, vocal pieces, or romances." And on exactly the same day, he received a similar offer from the firm of Schott, who apologized for their earlier neglect on the grounds that they had been publishing too much Beethoven! Schubert promptly offered Schott his E-flat Piano Trio, two string quartets and an assortment of piano pieces and songs. In fact, as often happened, both publishers proved hard-nosed bargainers after their tempting approaches. The offer from Schott came to nothing, while Probst finally knocked the price of the E-flat Piano Trio down to almost half of what Schubert felt it was worth.

At the end of March, Schubert ventured to put on the first public concert of his own works (something Beethoven had done from the time he first arrived in Vienna). "Franz Schubert's Invitation Concert" was held on March 26, 1828, in a room in "Zum roten Igel" ("House of the Red Hedgehog"), belonging to the Vienna Philharmonic Society.

Nicolò Paganini (1782–1840)

The program consisted of songs, choruses, including the popular *Ständchen* ("Serenade") for contralto solo, women's voices, and piano, a movement of a string quartet, and the E-flat Piano Trio (which lasts nearly fifty minutes). Schubert's friends thought the concert "glorious," and repaired afterward to the Snail Tavern "where we jubilated until midnight." But no reviews appeared in the papers. Fashionable Vienna was elsewhere, going wild over the latest phenomenon. The great Italian violin virtuoso Nicolò Paganini was triumphantly touring Europe. His Viennese concerts were soon sold out. "There is only one voice within our walls, and it cries 'Hear Paganini!'," reported a newspaper. Schubert went to hear him twice, once when the great wizard (a tall, gaunt figure, as famous for his many love affairs as for the incredible technical feats he could perform on the violin, and said by some to have sold his soul to the Devil) performed his Second Concerto. Schubert was more impressed by Paganini's lovely, singing tone than his amazing virtuosity. "I heard an angel sing in the Adagio," he wrote.

The same month, Schubert offered his last completed Symphony – know as the "Great C major" – to the Society of Music Lovers in Vienna; but in the event the Society turned it down on the grounds that it was too difficult – the players couldn't cope. In this work Schubert really did try to outdo Beethoven. It lasts nearly an hour in performance, and requires enormous stamina from the orchestral players – especially the strings! Although the composer Robert Schumann (at that time a boy of eighteen) later praised its "heavenly length," in some respects Schubert almost did overreach himself. His talent lay in his unerring ability to create flawless, small-scale gems, and to write beautiful melodies – something Beethoven would have envied. No other composer has ever written so many memorable tunes. But in the C major Symphony, Schubert followed Beethoven's principle of building up a huge symphonic structure from small motifs, held together by a powerful rhythmic drive – and sometimes he found it hard to keep his material under control!

Meanwhile, Schubert's publishers kept asking him for more piano music, to satisfy the ever-growing demand for music that wasn't too difficult, for people to play at home. As well as some shorter works, Schubert wrote three duet pieces – the fine Fantasy in F minor was dedicated to his pupil, Caroline Esterházy – and three piano sonatas, which were eventually published with a dedication to Schumann. "Purely and simply thunderstorms breaking forth, with Romantic rainbows over solemnly slumbering worlds," was how Schumann later described Schubert's piano music. As well as several church works, Schubert finished his last major group of songs; after his death these acquired the title *Schwanengesang* ("Swan Song"). This is not a song cycle as such, since it sets verses by three different poets, ranging in mood from the exquisite and justly famous *Ständchen* ("Serenade") to the terrifying *Der Doppelgänger* ("The Ghostly Double"), a setting of a poem by Heinrich Heine, in which a young man sees his "double" and realizes that the apparition foretells his own death.

Ständchen (Serenade) from "Schwanengesang"

Schubert himself had only a few more months to live. By September, his health was so poor that, on his doctor's advice, he moved in with his brother Ferdinand, who lived in an expanding suburb of Vienna, now the Kettenbrückengasse. But the newly built house was damp, hardly suitable for an invalid. "I've set a few songs by Heine of Hamburg . . . and have finally turned out a Quintet for 2 violins, 1 viola and 2 cellos. If by any chance any of these would suit you, let me know," wrote the modest composer to his skinflint publisher. This Quintet, in C major, was to be his instrumental swan song. Whereas similar pieces by Mozart use two violas (Mozart's favorite string instrument), Schubert adds depth by using two cellos. Many people consider the Quintet, in which all five instruments weave a mesh of

The house in the Kettenbrückengasse where Schubert died

he was confined to bed with typhus, nursed by his brother and his sister-in-law, and his little stepsister, Josefa. "I am ill," he wrote to Schober. "I have eaten nothing and drunk nothing for eleven days, and I can only stagger feebly from my bed to a chair and back again." On his deathbed, Schubert discovered who his true friends were. Josef von Spaun, his old schoolfellow and most devoted friend, continued to visit him, but Schober – for some reason – kept away. During his final delirium, Schubert kept calling out to Ferdinand not to leave him "in this corner under the earth." – "But you are in your own room, in your bed," replied his brother. – "No," said Schubert. "It is not true: Beethoven does not lie here." At three o'clock on November 19, Schubert turned to his brother. "Here, here is my end" he said.

He was buried two days later, close to his idol Beethoven, in the Währing cemetery. His grieving friends arranged a memorial service, and organized a fund to put up a monument to him (he had died leaving only debts). In 1830, the monument, bearing a bronze bust of the composer, was duly erected over the grave. It carries a brief, but telling, epitaph: "The art of music has buried here a rich possession, but even greater hopes."

the most ravishing, sensuous beauty, pierced with daggers of pain, to be Schubert's finest achievement. Like much of Schubert's music, it was not heard in public until many years after his death.

In October, Schubert felt well enough to make a three-day pilgrimage on foot to Haydn's grave at Eisenstadt, a distance of about 50 miles. He also completed a substantial virtuoso recital piece for Anna Milder-Hauptmann with piano accompaniment and clarinet obbligato, called *Der Hirt auf dem Felsen* ("The Shepherd on the Rock"). But when, at the end of the month, he visited his local tavern with his brother, he couldn't eat his fish. Within a fortnight

A bronze bust of Schubert

Glossary of Musical Terms

Symphony A large-scale orchestral piece, usually in four separate movements (Schubert's "Unfinished" Symphony has only two). The first and last were usually quick; the second slow, and the third was often a minuet (a graceful dance), or a scherzo (a fast piece, literally meaning "a joke").

Sonata A piece for one or two instruments (such as piano alone, or violin and piano), in up to four movements.

Chamber Music Pieces for a small but varied group of instruments, each playing an individual part.

Trio A piece of chamber music for three instruments. A piano trio consisted of piano, violin, and cello; a string trio of violin, viola, and cello.

Quartet A piece of chamber music for four instruments (a string quartet consisted of two violins, viola, and cello).

Quintet A piece of chamber music for five instruments (a string quintet normally had two violins, two violas, and one cello; but Schubert's Quintet uses two cellos instead of two violas).

Octet A piece of chamber music for eight instruments.

Nonet A piece of chamber music for nine instruments.

Variations A form used for piano pieces, or for movements of larger works, in which a simple tune is treated in a series of different ways.

Opera A drama set to music, usually in several acts.

Singspiel A lighter form of opera, sung in German, with spoken dialogue between the music.

Incidental Music Music written to accompany a stage play (usually just for instruments).

Mass A musical setting of the Catholic church service, in Latin.

Motet A shorter piece of music for church use.

Song Cycle A sequence of songs, linked together both by the text and the music.

List of Works

Stage Works

17, including *Die Zauberharfe* ("The Magic Harp," 1820), *Alfonso und Estrella* (1821–2), *Fierabras* (1823), *Rosamunde* (incidental music, 1823).

Vocal Music

6 masses, in F, G, B flat, C, A flat, E flat; 7 *Salve regina*, 2 *Stabat mater*, many other motets, etc.
About 130 choruses, partsongs, and cantatas for various combinations of voices.
Over 600 songs, including around 70 settings of Goethe poems, and the song cycles *Die schöne Müllerin* (20 songs, 1823) and *Winterreise* (24 songs, 1827), both to poems by Wilhelm Müller.

Orchestral Music

8 "completed" symphonies, No.1 in D (1813), No.2 in B flat (1814–15), No.3 in D (1815), No.4 in C minor ("Tragic," 1816), No.5 in B flat (1816), No.6 in C (1817–18), No.8 in B minor ("Unfinished," 1822), No.9 in C ("Great C major," 1825–6); sketches for several others.
8 overtures; 9 overtures to stage works,

including *Rosamunde*; 1 violin concerto (1816); Rondo in A for violin and orchestra (1816); Polonaise in B flat for violin and orchestra (1816).

Chamber Music

6 pieces for wind and strings, including Nonet for winds in E flat minor ("A Little Mourning Music," 1813); Octet for clarinet, horn, bassoon, 2 violins, viola, cello, and double bass (1824).

4 piano trios; Quintet ("Trout") for piano, violin, viola, cello, and double bass (1819); 4 violin sonatas; 1 arpeggione sonata; *Rondo brillant* in B minor for violin and piano, *Fantasie* in C for violin and piano. 15 string quartets, including No.12 ("Quartettsatz") in C minor (1824), No.13 in A minor (1824), No.14 in D minor ("Death and the Maiden," 1824), No.15 in G (1826), various other dances and movements for string quartet; String Quintet in C (1828); 2 string trios (1816–17).

Piano Music

About 35 pieces for piano duet, including Sonata in C ("Grand Duo", 1824), *Divertissement à l'hongroise* (1824), *Fantasie* in F minor (1828).

Over 40 large-scale pieces for solo piano, including 20 sonatas and the "Wanderer" Fantasy in C (1822); many shorter piano pieces, including *Moments Musicaux* (1823–4), Impromptus (Op.90, Op.142, 1827); over 400 dances for keyboard.

Picture Credits

The author and publishers have made every effort to identify the owners of the pictures used in this publication; they apologize for any inaccuracies and would like to thank the following
(*a: left, b: right*):

Historisches Museen der Stadt Wien 8, 13b, 22, 31a, 31b, 32b, 37.
Sammlungen der Gesellschaft der Musikfreunde in Wien 13c, 15b, 17, 24, 27b.
Bild-Archiv der Österreichischen Nationalbibliothek Wien 20b.
Graphische Sammlung Albertina, Vienna 39.
Musée du Louvre, Paris 29a.
The Tate Gallery, London 29b.
The Royal College of Music, London frontispiece, 38.
ET Archive 3, 11, 12, 19, 25, 27a, 30a, 32a, 35, 40, 46a (Historisches Museen der Stadt Wien), 5 (Schubert Museum, Vienna), 20a (Gesellschaft der Musikfreunde in Wien).
Author's collection 4a, 4b, 6, 7, 9, 10, 13a, 15a, 30b, 33a, 33b, 34a, 42.

The cover shows a portrait of Schubert by Rieder against an engraving of a café in a Viennese park (Historisches Museen der Stadt Wien, both reproduced by permission of ET Archive).

The author wishes to acknowledge her debt to many sources, including *The Great Composers: Schubert* by John Reed (Faber & Faber, 1978), *The Master Musicians: Schubert* by John Reed (J.M. Dent & Sons, 1987), *Franz Schubert* (Grove 6), *Schubert: A Documentary Biography* by O.E. Deutsch (J.M. Dent & Sons, 1946).

VIKING
Published by the Penguin Group
Viking Penguin, a division of Penguin Books USA Inc., 375 Hudson Street, New York, New York 10014, U.S.A.
Penguin Books Ltd, 27 Wrights Lane, London W8 5TZ, England
Penguin Books Australia Ltd, Ringwood, Victoria, Australia
Penguin Books Canada Ltd, 2801 John Street, Markham, Ontario, Canada L3R 1B4
Penguin Books (N.Z.) Ltd, 182—190 Wairau Road, Auckland 10, New Zealand

Penguin Books Ltd, Registered Offices: Harmondsworth, Middlesex, England

First published in Great Britain by Faber Music Ltd in association with Faber and Faber Ltd, 1991

First American edition published in 1991

10 9 8 7 6 5 4 3 2 1

Library of Congress Catalog Card Number: 91—50213

ISBN 0-670-84172-2

Printed in Spain

Set in Sabon Roman